MY FIRST BOOK

ALGERIA

ALL ABOUT ALGERIA FOR KIDS

GLOBED
CHILDREN BOOKS

Interior and cover Design: Daniel Day
Editor: Margaret Bam

For My Sons, Daniel, David and Jude

Oran, Algeria

Algeria

Algeria is a **country**.

A country is land that is controlled by a **single government**. Countries are also called **nations, states, or nation-states**.

Countries can be **different sizes**. Some countries are big and others are small.

Sahara Desert, Algeria

Where Is Algeria?

Algeria is located in the continent of Africa.

A continent is a massive area of land that is separated from others by water or other natural features.

Algeria is situated in North Africa.

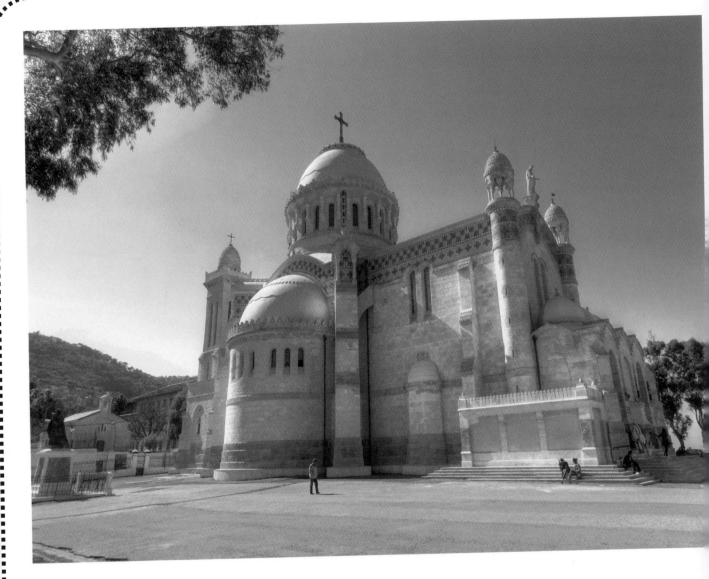

Algiers, Algeria

Capital

The capital of Algeria is Algiers.

Algiers is located in the **northern part** of the country.

Algiers is the largest city in Algeria.

Berbero-Roman ruins, Djemila, Algeria

Regions

Algeria is divided into 58 wilayas (provinces).

Some of the wilayas of Algeria are:

Algérois, Aurès Mountains, Constantinois, Gourara, Hautes Plaines, Hodna, Hoggar Mountains, Grande Kabylie, Petite Kabylie, Basse Kabylie, Eastern Kabylie, The M'zab, Mitidja, Annaba region, The Saoura, Titteri, The Tell, Tidikelt, Trara Mountains, Touat, Oranie, South Oranie, Chelif River valley, The Dahra Range, The Ouarsenis, The Zibans, The Algerian Sahara, Grand Erg Oriental and Grand Erg Occidental, Souf, Tassill n'Ajjer and Tanezrouft.

Population

Algeria has a population of around **44 million people** making it the 9th most populated country in Africa and the 32nd most populated country in the world.

Algiers, Algeria

Size

Algeria is **2,381,741 square kilometres** making it the 10th largest country in the world by area. Algeria is the largest country in Africa.

Languages

The official languages of Algeria are **Arabic and Tamazight.** The Arabic language is spoken by hundreds of million people around the world.

French is also spoken in Algeria.

Here are a few Algerian phrases and sayings
- **Salam** - Hello
- **Sbah l-khir** - Good morning
- **Mrahba bik** - Welcome

Fort of Santa Cruz

Attractions

There are lots of interesting places to see in Algeria.

Some beautiful places to visit in Algeria are

- Martyr's Memorial
- Botanical Garden Hamma
- Church of Notre Dame of Africa
- Fort of Santa Cruz
- Sidi M'Cid Bridge
- Amir Abdel Kader Mosque

Algerian man

History of Algeria

People have lived in Algeria for a very long time. In fact, evidence of the early human occupation of Algeria is demonstrated by the discovery of 1.8 million year old Oldowan stone tools.

Algeria has been linked to many civilizations, empires and dynasties such as Vandals, Byzantines, Umayyad, Phoenicians, Carthaginians and Romans.

Algeria gained full independence in 1962.

Moroccan Tea with Oriental Algerian sweets

Customs in Algeria

Algeria has many fascinating customs and traditions.

- **Algerians are known for their hospitality, especially toward guests. It is common for Algerians to invite visitors or friends into their home for cups of tea and good company.**
- **Elders are given extra respect and consideration in Algerian culture. When attending a social gathering, it is customary to greet the eldest first.**

Music of Algeria

There are many different music genres in Algeria such as **Raï, Chaabi, Andalusi classical music, Zindalii, Ma'luf and Chaabi.**

Some notable Algerian musicians include
- **Soolking**
- **Cheb Mami**
- **Rachid Taha**
- **Zaho**
- **Lounès Matoub**
- **Idir**

Cous cous

Food of Algeria

Algerian food is known for being tasty, delicious and flavoursome.

The national dish of Algeria is **Couscous,** which is composed of small pellets of steamed semolina topped with meat, vegetables, and various spices.

Chakchouka

Food of Algeria

Some popular dishes in Algeria include

- **Chakchouka**
- **Couscous**
- **Rechta**
- **Dobara**
- **Berkoukes**
- **Chorba Frik**
- **Harira**

El Jedid Mosque, Algeria

Weather in Algeria

Algeria has a **Mediterranean climate** characterised by mild, rainy winters and hot, sunny summers.

The hottest month in Algeria is **August.**

Dromedary Camel in Algeria

Animals of Algeria

There are many wonderful animals in Algeria.

Here are some animals that live in Algeria.

- Wild boars
- Jackals
- Gazelles
- Panthers
- Leopards
- Cheetahs
- Camel

The Djamaa El Djazair mosque

Mosques

There are many beautiful mosques in Algeria which is one of the reasons why so many people visit this beautiful country every year.

Here are some of Algeria's mosques
- Ketchaoua Mosque
- The Djamaa El Djazair mosque
- Amir Abdel Kader Mosque
- Abdullah Bin Salem Mosque

Football with Algeria Flag

Sports in Algeria

Sports play an integral part in Algerian culture. The most popular sport is Football.

Here are some of famous sportspeople from Algeria

- Abderrahmane Morceli - Athletics
- Sakina Boutamine - Athletics
- Fatima-Zohra Oukazi - Volleyball
- Abdelmalek Slahdji - Handball

Travelling to Algeria

Famous

Many successful people hail from Algeria.

Here are some notable Algerian figures

- **Islam Slimani – Footballer**
- **Emir Abdelkader – Leader**
- **Ahmed Ben Bella – Politician**
- **Rachid Taha – Singer**

Something Extra...

As a little something extra, we are going to share some lesser known facts about Algeria

- **Algeria is home to the largest swath of the Sahara Desert.**
- **Algeria has won the Africa Cup of Nations football championship twice.**

Ghardaia, Algeria

Words From the Author

We hope that you enjoyed learning about the wonderful country of Algeria.

Algeria is a country rich in culture and beauty, with lots of wonderful places to visit and people to meet.

We hope you continue to learn more about this wonderful nation. If you enjoyed this book, consider leaving a review!

With Love

Printed in Great Britain
by Amazon

38962660R00027